Writing from a place of personal experience, Andrews captures the depth and debilitating nature of grief. More important, she offers simple things that all of us can do to help those around us struggling to come to terms with the loss of someone dear to us. The worst thing is to do nothing. Sometimes, it's as simple as bringing soup. *Please Bring Soup* is a necessary book, one that should be shared with friends and family who are grieving; it will help the rest of us to better acknowledge (not ignore) and validate the reality of the process.

–**Jim Baumer**, author of *Moxie: Maine in a Bottle*

When her beloved husband Jim died suddenly, Linda Andrews suffered one of the most difficult life losses imaginable. Over the subsequent days and months, she followed her heart and her heartache through the chaotic path of grief, facing every painful emotion that comes in the wake of deep loss. Sustained by the steadfast love and support of her family and friends, she also began writing her way through her grief—not only as a channel for her own healing, but for the comfort and hope it might one day offer to another person grieving or helping someone through loss. In *Please Bring Soup*, Linda shares her story with extraordinary honesty and vulnerability, offering profound life lessons about life and loss and the power of love. It is a book for everyone who will ever face the death of a loved one: in other words, each and every one of us.

-**Marian Claxt**

GW00646268

Please Bring Soup
To Comfort Me While I Grieve

Linda Andrews

Please Bring Soup: To Comfort Me While I Grieve / by
Linda Andrews
ISBN: 978-0-9968227-0-1

Contents

This book is dedicated to my husband Jim and the life we shared. I will miss you for the rest of my life.

Introduction

Prior to September of 2011, life was good. My husband and I had been married for thirty one years. We raised identical twin sons who were successful and respectful young men. We were incredibly proud of them. We had three young granddaughters whom we loved and adored.

We had a log cabin on a lake that served as a get-away not just for us but also for our family and friends. Spending time there was relaxing and joyful whether it was just the two of us or a big family get-together.

Then came September of 2011

On Friday, September second, my Dad, a very important figure in my life, passed away after a short illness at the remarkable age of ninety one. My mom died three years before him after a long illness and also on a Friday. For ten years, my sister, brother, and I were immersed in our parents' care. In the end, we watched both of them with-er away and die. We were emotionally and physically exhausted. Through all the grief and sadness of losing my parents, my husband, Jim, was there for me. He supported me and was understanding when we had to cancel plans because mom or dad needed me. It was a long journey, and we would need time to heal.

Once again at my dad's funeral, my husband was by my side holding my hand and comforting me. I remember telling him that day how handsome he looked in his suit. I remember thinking that now would be our time. I would schedule a get-away for the two of us. I wanted to thank him for all the love and support he had given me while I cared for my parents.

But that was just not in the plan. Nine days after my dad's funeral, I was having a particularly sad day. I remember that night my husband put his arms around me and said, "You are going to be all right" How prophetic those words would become.

The very next day, he died. It happened on a **Friday**!

My world was turned upside down. How could this be happening? I just buried my Dad nine days ago. The pain that followed was unimaginable. The things people said or did not say hurt so much. I realized early on that so many people in our society are ill equipped to deal with grief.

Therefore, I decided to write a book. I enjoy writing as a way to share my ideas with others. If even one person is comforted by my story, or if I can help someone know what to say or not say to someone grieving, I will have succeeded.

This book is for anyone who is grieving or supporting someone who has suffered a loss. It is about what worked and did not work for me, a woman suffering the loss of two very special men in her life in a two week span.

While grief is personal, and we all navigate through it in our own way, I have discovered on my journey that we share some similarities. We understand how deep and unbearable the pain is. We know that we could never have imagined just how hard this full time grief job would be. We know that when we talk and share with others who have experienced loss, they "get it." I became a member of a "Grief Club" that I did not sign up for. I l also learned that you do not have to go very far to find other members of this club.

It is my hope this book will offer some thoughts that will help you personally, or enable you to help someone you love. Perhaps, my story will resonate with you, and bring you or your loved one even one moment of peace.

Imagine a Job Posting That Reads Like This

Start Date: Immediately
Hours: 24/7
Salary: None
Vacations: None
Days off: None

Requirements: Must be able to feel sad and lonely most of the time, must be able to cry often, must be able to go without sleep for days; must be able to feel vulnerable, confused, and indecisive.

Timeline: As many years as it takes.

Now you are thinking, "Who in their right mind would apply for this job? No one right?

Now imagine this is **your** job!

In the Blink of An Eye

On Friday September 16, 2011, I was working in my office and looking forward to the weekend and spending time with my family.

I was having lunch with a co-worker when the call came. Someone on the other end of the phone said "Your husband has been in an accident and it is serious." "Oh my God," I shouted as my stomach churned.

How could this be? I must get to the hospital. My co-worker, Elaine, says," I will drive you."

On the way, I say to her, "This cannot be happening" I just lost my dad two weeks ago; this has to be a mistake. I cannot take any more bad news.

I am thinking that when I get to the hospital, he will be hooked to machines and have lots of tubes but he will be all right. He has to be all right.

I call my son Sean and tell him his Dad has been in an accident and it is serious. He responds, "I'm on my way."

The doctor is there to greet me in the ER. He says," It was not an accident; he had a cardiac arrest and his truck went off the road. He is gone." I want to say, "Take back those words you horrible person, I cannot breathe, I am in shock, this cannot be real" My son is there, his wife, Michelle, is there. We cry-We hug. We are shocked and confused. This cannot be happening.

They lead us to a room reserved for occasions like this. They tell us we need to say goodbye. Goodbye? I am not ready to say goodbye. I saw him this morning; he was drinking his coffee, he was reading the newspaper, and he called me twice this morning. He went to the gym. You do not die on your way home from the gym. This has to be a bad dream, take it back, and tell us you made a mistake.

My son has to call his brother Brian. He and his girlfriend, Lauren, are expected home later today to spend the weekend at our cabin on the lake; we would join them there on Saturday.

Brian says "You're kidding" when he gets the call. Sean does not understand why his brother says that but of course he too is in shock, he cannot be receiving this call, he is just walking around his house not knowing what to do.

We are not there to comfort him, to hug him, to cry with him. He has to get home to see his dad. He calls his girlfriend and says we have to leave now. "My Dad just died" How can he be saying those words? How can he travel two and a half hours knowing what he is coming home to? This cannot be. This is all wrong.

The hospital staff and my daughter-in-law are calling family and friends. The hospital social worker says you need your family here. I am numb. I let them do what they think is best. We have to call his sister Jane. They are very close. She will be in shock. When she arrives at the hospital, she cannot believe it. She also talked to him on the phone this morning. My brother Richard, my sister Patricia, and my niece Jill arrive to support us. No one can believe this is happening.

When Brian arrives from Boston, he, Sean and I go to see their dad. We do not want to say good-bye; we have so much left to do. This is my husband, this is their dad. How can we manage without this very important person? The idea of it is unimaginable.

What do we do now? Plan a funeral? How can we? This was not supposed to happen. My boys still need their dad. He is their mentor, their teacher, their historian. I still need him. I do not want to spend the rest of my life alone. We had plans for our future.

When we all got up this morning, we did not think we would be spending our evening planning a funeral. We are just being led through the steps. Are we really doing this? Or are we in a movie? Are we all acting? Will someone say "cut" and will he then be back? He looks fine….not a scratch. We tell him, "Get up, this is not funny, we need you." But that does not happen.

Our Home

When we arrive at the house, his things are there; his coffee cup from this morning, his reading glasses next to the newspaper.

Seeing these things hurts so much. I realize I will never see him in this house, our home, again. I will never see him reading the paper or drinking his coffee. The simple things he did every single day will no longer happen.

From "Healing after Loss" September 16 entry:

"But I am no more I,

Nor is my house now my house"

Thankfully, Brian and Lauren are in the house with me. I could not be alone right now. I cannot sleep, eat, or even think. I am in shock. I am angry with the universe.

Somehow the hours of sleeplessness go by and now it is morning. I feel lost and unsure as how to proceed. What do I do next? Brian takes charge and calls my niece, Jill. She and my sister arrive with coffee, and food. Sean and Michelle come by so we can all be together. We must decide what to do next.

My husband's sister calls and says. "This is just unbearable." I tell her to come and be with us. We all need to be together today. Later, her husband Walter, and their daughter Rebecca join us.

The phone keeps ringing but I cannot speak to anyone. My sons are taking the calls.

My brother Richard and his wife Jackie bring more food and see to it that everyone gets dinner. I am not able to do a thing. I am still numb. I eat a few morsels of food. I am too sad. My son brings my granddaughters to the house. The four year old asks for Beepa, as he was known to the girls. Jim was so attached to them. It is breaking my heart to think that they will never see him again; he will never again play with them in our home. He loved them so much! It hurts to think about it.

From my journal:

This is so hard. I miss him so much and want him in this house. Coming to terms with the idea of that never happening is more than I can bear. I am working so hard and expending so much energy to get myself through each day that it is really affecting me physically. It is energy I do not have in store.

The Wake

One thing we knew is that my husband would not want a traditional wake or a funeral. At my dad's wake, my husband shared with our sons that he did not want any of "this" He did not want an obituary and he did not want a service.

We were still in shock over the sudden loss however we knew we had to honor his wishes to the best of our ability. We decided that we would greet people at the funeral home for a two hour period. We hoped he would understand that we needed to do that.

That Sunday was a blur. Somehow everyone pulled together and made posters with photos. The boys and I chose their dad's favorite music to play at the wake. We would forego the traditional funeral music and listen to Bob Dylan, Warren Zevon, and Bob Seger. We knew he would appreciate that. We arrived at the funeral home with our close family. We were all very nervous, sad and dazed. None of us could believe we had all been here just nine days ago saying good-bye to my dad.

When my dad was ill and dying, my husband was there supporting me and my family. I never got the chance to really thank him for that. I imagined us taking a trip together. We went through so much with my Dad and three years before that, my Mom. That trip is just a lost dream now.

Why did this happen? I am thinking it is still not too late for someone to tell me it was all a mistake. Please just bring him back. We miss him, we need him and we love him.

Today my son Sean said, "I just want him here one more day Mom. I want to tell him how much he meant to me. I want to tell him what a good job he did bringing us up and thank him for all he taught us." It breaks my heart to hear this. I am so sad for his loss. He is my son and I do not want to see him in pain.

We are in awe over the number of people that come to greet us at the funeral home. There is a line out the door. We are honored that so many people cared enough to come on this very sad and horrific day. It had a huge impact on us. Family, friends, and co-workers of Jim's, and mine as well as friends and co-workers of my sons came from near and far. We were touched by this expression of love and support. We could not help but wonder, "What would he think of this?"

From our neighbor Alan:

Jim was a good neighbor and friend. I will remember Jim for his unique insights and a passion for conversation that mirrored mine. In my discussions with Jim, it was clear that he loved his family. It was always with great pride that he spoke of his sons and hardly a conversation went by that at least one of their names wasn't spoken. I think that Jim would wish us to open the door to a celebration of his life, rather than sorrow, and so I am sure his greatest satisfaction would be that we might simply be richer people for having known him.

The Service

Again in keeping with my husband's wishes, we did our best to honor him. There would be no official service at the funeral home, no church service, but instead a family only gathering at the cemetery. He would be next to his parents and other relatives.

It was a difficult and sad time. My sons and I were struggling with the thought of having to say goodbye. Sean read a poem which was not easy for him. We were still in shock.

From the Book *Healing After Loss Daily Meditations for Working Through Grief* by Martha Whitmore Hickman:

There is no more ridiculous custom than the one that makes you express sympathy once and for all on a given day to a person whose sorrow will endure as long as his life. Such grief, felt in such a way, is always "present," it is never too late to talk about it, never repetitious to mention it again.

After the gathering, we head to my husband's sister's house to be together. It was a warm sunny day so we sat outside. At some point people were talking and laughing and just being normal but nothing was normal for me. I just could not be comfortable with any of this. Why wasn't he here laughing and joking and giving Jane a hard time? They were so close and enjoyed teasing each other. She will miss him so much.

I Am Alone Now

Tonight will be my first night in the house alone. My sister offers to stay with me but I tell her I need to do this. I cannot sleep of course; I twist and turn and cannot keep the sad thoughts out of my head. I cannot sleep in the bedroom. As a matter of fact, I have a hard time even being upstairs in the house. I am sleeping or rather trying to sleep on the couch. The couch would become my resting spot for an entire year.

He Is Sitting On My Shoulder

I feel like I have a sad movie playing over and over in my head and no matter how much I want to turn the movie off, if even for a little while, the remote just does not work. It keeps playing over and over and over.

My husband is sitting right there on my shoulder and I cannot move him. Part of me does not want to move him because I feel I owe him this. I must honor him, his life, and our life together. This will be an exhausting journey.

From my journal*:*

The sad movie is playing in my head. It is amazing how heavy sadness is and how all-consuming it can be. It takes over your whole being. There is no way to control it, only to manage it from time to time.

A Random Stranger

When we were all gathered in the Emergency Room of the hospital on that fateful day, the social worker handed me a piece of paper. On it was the name and number of a woman who had called the hospital.

The social worker explained that this woman, a random stranger, was on the scene when my husband's truck went off the road after his cardiac arrest. She and others on the scene broke the window in his truck to get to him and try to help him. She wanted me to know that and to have her number in the event I wanted to talk to her. I put the number in my purse as it was not something I was prepared to think about on that sad and devastating day.

Two days later, the woman appeared at the wake. The funeral director led her to us as we were greeting people. She was overcome with emotion. I actually found myself comforting her. She wanted me to know that she was there with my husband, that he was not alone. She explained that she tried to administer CPR and was apologetic that she could not save him. She brought me beautiful flowers.

For a while, I was unsure or incapable of knowing how to feel about this random stranger. There were days I thought I might call her. Did she have details that might help me understand what happened to my husband? Did I want this information? Would it help me to know the details? I struggled with these questions and ultimately did not call her.

But I frequently think about the random stranger who tried to save my husband. I think about how this event must have changed her. Is she all right? How did that day affect her life? If I saw her today, I would hug her and I would thank her for her unbelievable act of kindness.

The Cards and Flowers

Each day when more cards and flowers arrived, it touched my heart. Reading the personal notes in the cards meant so much to me and my sons. We were moved by the fact that people took the time to write a note in the card. Unless someone has experienced this type of loss, it is very hard to appreciate how much the simple act of receiving a card can mean to someone who is grieving. Each day when I went to the mailbox, I worried there would be no more cards.

People told me not to worry about sending thank you notes however, it was very important to me to acknowledge those who took the time and effort to reach out to me and my sons with cards and gifts. I made sure my family and friends were watering the plants; caring for the flowers, and planting and caring for the "Seeds of Life" magnolia tree I received.

I do not believe I can adequately express the gratitude I

felt when I received these kind and thoughtful gifts of sympathy. When you are feeling vulnerable, it is nice to know people care enough to write a personal note. When someone shared a story about my husband, it was heartwarming. Even when people shared a funny story, it was good to know they appreciated his very unique sense of humor.

Though my husband knew how much he meant to his family and how much we loved him, I believe he would be touched to know just how much he meant to the people around him and how he impacted their lives.

From a friend Jim worked out with at the Wellness Center:

I knew Jim as a man of high principles and pride. He held himself to a high standard of conduct, and expected similar from others. I continue to frequent the Wellness Center, but there is a difference, and emptiness. I sometimes feel Jim's presence there, and the empty feeling leaves.

Society's Response to Grief

When it comes to the topic of grief, many people are uncomfortable and unprepared to know what to say or do. Some people try to say the right thing and others just avoid the whole situation. The effect on the person who is grieving is devastating; feelings of pain, hurt, anger and disappointment prevail. People who are grieving are not in a position to understand this flaw in the human spirit.

I experienced this last September when I lost my dad and again two weeks later when my husband suddenly and unexpectedly died. It was overwhelming. Never in my life have I felt so vulnerable. I was not prepared for the intensity of the sadness, pain, and despair. My heart was broken and there was pain in my soul. A quote from the movie "Meet Joe Black" sent to me by Lauren describes it best:

Multiply it by infinity and take it to the depth of forever and you will still just have a glimpse of how it feels.

When you are grieving, you hope people will not hold you accountable for what you say. You are hurt, sad, yet out there in the world. You feel raw. You cannot understand why the rest of the world is going on with their day to day life. After all, you just lost one, or in my case, two of the most important people in your life and the world should come to a standstill. While intellectually you know that does not make sense, your heart does not understand.

You look fairly normal so the world does not know what you are going through. You would like to wear a sign that says "Don't mind me....I am grieving."

From my journal:

This process is earth shattering and unpredictable and can blindside you when you least expect it. It is like someone moved in and took control of your mind and body. They took all your energy and drained it and then placed you in the world and expected you to go about your life. It is disturbing and as if the real you is standing on the sidelines watching all this happen. You do not like it but you do not have a say in the matter....you have no voice and you have no strength to fight off this alien called grief that has moved in and taken over.

What You Say or Do Not Say Hurts

Choosing the right words to say to someone who is grieving can be difficult however some words are more helpful than others.

"How are you," is a normal everyday greeting, yet it can be very upsetting to hear when you are grieving. You just suffered a loss so how the heck do they think you are? It just does not make sense to people that are grieving.

One alternative is to ask, "How is today going?" When you are grieving, it is about getting through one day at a time and each day can be very different. When someone asks this question, they are acknowledging that you are not okay and they genuinely want to know how you are coping.

From Lauren:

How are the day-to-day tasks coming? Is there anything that's been particularly hard lately? Or a better question–has anything made you smile this week?

When I received this from Lauren, it really did make me try to think of even one moment that made me smile, and for that I was grateful.

One of the phrases that troubled me the most was "Some people just don't know what to say." When I would express my disappointment that people were ignoring me and I received this comment in return, I felt like it was about the other person and so I should feel sorry for them that they are unprepared to know what to say to me.

In reality, all I could think of was how unprepared I was to deal with the sudden and unexpected loss of my husband so soon after the loss of my dad. I wanted to say. "If it is hard for you, then imagine what it is like on my end."

A friend of mine who lost her sister shared a story with me. She said the day of her sister's wake one of her friend's called to say, "I cannot go to the wake, it is just too hard for me." My friend was speechless. She was unprepared to manage her loss and could have used the support of her friend on that day.

Indeed, sometimes there are extenuating circumstances. If someone has very recently also suffered a loss, it truly can be too hard for them to be in a funeral home. This was the case with one of my friends, and I truly did understand that.

Many fellow grievers shared with me that as devastated

as they were on the day of the wake, they remembered everyone who came and also everyone who did not.

If only people realized that saying, "I just don't know what to say," works. It is real and it is true. Other words that work include:

"I am so sorry."

"I cannot imagine what you are going through."

"It is unimaginable."

"There are no words."

"You are in my heart."

Another idea is just to give a hug. A hug is better than words for some. A young woman I met told me she lost her mother when she was just fourteen years old. At the service, many of the adults said things that just did not make sense to her like, "She is in a better place." It was one of her fourteen year old classmates that had the biggest impact on her. She did not use words; she simply gave her friend a hug.

At the wake, I cannot tell you how many people said to me "Let me know if there is anything I can do." While their intentions were good, it put the responsibility on me. So in my worst most terrible time, I have to think of something you can do and then call you and let you know what that is. People do not realize that simply making a phone call in the early days is very difficult.

A friend of mine who had lost her eighteen year old daughter became an incredible source of comfort to me. When her daughter died suddenly and unexpectedly, people said things to her like: "At least you have another daughter," and, "She is in a better place." The pain that comes with hearing those words is difficult to describe.

At her daughter's wake, someone approached her at the photo display and said, "Introduce me to your daughter." That was a very wise and compassionate person. My friend remembers that kind gesture to this day.

It is important to remember that when someone experiences loss, it becomes about them, not you. Even if you have experienced loss yourself, today it is about them. Even if you think you understand just how they feel, today is not the time or place to express that. There will be a time and a place for you to share your story and when the time is right, it will undoubtedly be a gift to your friend.

There is no doubt that knowing what to say to someone who is grieving is challenging. We will sometimes say the perfect thing and sometimes not. We will rely on the griever to guide us and we will accept their guidance with grace and dignity. We will look in our rear view mirror and ask ourselves, "How can I do that better next time?" because one thing we know for sure is that there will be a next time.

The View From Within

From the outside, people who are grieving may appear to be okay. If you could see inside, it would be a different story.

If someone has a gaping wound on their leg, you can look at it and say, "That looks so painful." When you see them again and notice that the wound is healing you can comment about how much better it looks. It is easy to know what to say in that situation.

Unfortunately people cannot see a broken heart. They cannot know how it feels unless they too have suffered a profound loss. Because they cannot see it, they may not acknowledge it. They may try to avoid having a conversation with you or worse yet avoid you altogether. In their mind, that seems like the right thing to do. If only they knew the effect that had on you: the hurt, the disappointment, and the feeling that you have a contagious disease.

To avoid these uncomfortable moments, you mask your broken heart. It is like putting a bandage on the gaping wound on your leg. People cannot see it, so they do not ask or comment. They just assume you are alright. Some days you do this because you know that just being around you is a difficult task for the outside world.

At the wake I remember saying to some of my friends, "Please don't forget me." That gives you some idea of just how vulnerable I was feeling.

Lauren's Gift:

This piece embodies the dark times as well as the light and hope that are yet to come. The shells represent the heart, though it has been broken, still exists—the shattered pieces have just have been put back together differently.

We All Manage Grief Differently

My grief counselor told me that how you respond to any adversity in your life will be how you respond to grief.

During my immediate grief, I absolutely had to be surrounded by people. For a long time I could not get through a day unless people were around me. If I was alone too long with my feelings of sadness, panic overcame me. It was unchartered territory for me. I was exhausted, unable to sleep or eat. I did not know what to do with myself or my grief.

From my journal:

I am like a warrior in the battle of grief. Some days I can fight off the bad thoughts but some days the bad thoughts win.

As the months wore on, I learned that sometimes I could manage my grief on my own, that sometimes I needed to manage it on my own.

To my husband Jim, from my journal:

Today I am crying and grieving by myself. I feel a need to hold onto my thoughts for some reason and miss you privately today. I am having a hard time understanding why you cannot be here with me. I love you. I miss you. This is so unfair.

Everyone's response to grief is different. There is no right or wrong way to grieve; there is just your way.

From *Grief Therapy*:

Give yourself time to grieve. It may take several years just to accept the finality of a loss, that someone is gone forever and even more to work through your emotions.

Grief Education

Grief and loss are a part of life. All of us will eventually experience profound loss and the sadness and pain that accompany it. We need to do more as a society to address grief in schools, in the workplace, and in the community. Writing this book is my way to contribute.

In July of 2011, a co-worker of mine lost her twenty seven year old daughter suddenly and tragically. I was on vacation when this happened and when I heard about it, I knew I must call her. I could not begin to imagine what she was going through. I had to work up the courage to make that phone call. I tried to think of what I might say. What would even make sense to say? The first two times I called, she did not answer. I was actually relieved. This gave me more time to think of something appropriate to say. On my third attempt, she answered the phone. It turns out, all that came out of my mouth was "I am so sorry and I cannot imagine such a loss." She talked, I listened and somehow we got through the conversation. I knew it meant a lot to her to hear from me and I knew that I did something very important that day.

Two months later, my world fell apart. My expression of sympathy to my co-worker would now become even more significant.

If calling someone to express your sympathy is too difficult, you can send a text, or an e-mail. Sometimes that is actually easier for the griever as talking on the phone can be so emotional. If I was able to take the call, I did but everyone understood that I may not answer the phone. It was still comforting to know people were thinking of me.

We have so many communication options available to us in this day and age, maybe too many. A co-worker of mine asked for my input one day. She said she was not sure how to respond to the news on social media that her friend had suffered a loss. She said it did not feel like the right venue to address grief. My suggestion was to make it personal and private no matter what venue she chose. I told her how much personal notes and cards meant to me and my sons, that going to the mailbox and seeing cards there lifted my spirits.

Hearing from people no matter what the method keeps you going. Knowing people are acknowledging that this is the worst time of your life means so much. I was honored that she asked for and appreciated my input that day. It reminded me to keep writing my story because if people were reaching out to me and asking for my input now, then imagine how many more people I could reach with a book.

Are You Getting Everything You Need?

This question is complex in its simplicity. The day my husband died, I had a hair appointment scheduled at a salon I had only visited a few times. Needless to say, I missed that appointment.

Many weeks later, when I got the courage to go out in public, I made an appointment with my stylist. I thought perhaps having someone do something nurturing for me would be comforting. Indeed, Camden gave me an extra-long and luxurious scalp massage that day. She knew I needed that. It turns out she was a very compassionate young lady and listened to my story.

At some point, she said, "Are you getting everything you need?" That question was different than any other I had been asked. It really made me think. To me, it represented concern for me and an opportunity to think about what I did need. After all, in the early stages when you are so vulnerable, getting what you need is exceedingly important.

Sometimes Even a Stranger Can Make You Feel Better

When I called the telephone company to cancel my husband's cell phone, I broke down just talking about it. The customer service agent, a total stranger, said "Ma'am, I don't know you but if I were there, I would give you a hug."

It might be a total stranger or someone you least expect that says something kind and compassionate to you and helps you feel better for just one moment. Treasure that gift.

From Henri J. M. Nouwen:

When we honestly ask ourselves which person in our lives
means the most to us, we often find that it is those
who, instead of giving much advice,
solutions, or cures, have chosen rather to share our pain
and touch our wounds with a gentle and tender hand.

The friend who can be silent with us in a moment of despair
or confusion, who can stay with us in an hour of grief and
bereavement,
who can tolerate not knowing, not curing, not healing
and face with us the reality of our powerlessness,
that is a friend who cares.

There Are Stages

The five stages of grief first described by Dr. Elisabeth Kubler-Ross in her book, *On Death and Dying* include: denial, anger, bargaining, depression, and acceptance.

When I was in nursing school in Boston, I had the opportunity to hear her speak. Now, many years later, I had the opportunity to experience firsthand the five stages of grief.

DENIAL: This is when we just do not want to believe our loved one has died. Nothing makes sense to us and we are in shock and denial. People often wonder how any of us get through the wake and the funeral. They wonder how we are able to smile and laugh a little during that time. It is because none of it is real to us. We are just going through the motions. In our minds we are still convinced it did not happen and they will be back. Denial gets us through the early days.

From Lauren:

I really can't believe tomorrow it will be 4 weeks. It's a very unnerving and scary feeling that your whole entire life can become so unrecognizable in one moment. I obviously don't know firsthand how I'd react, but for some reason I think I might feel like I was watching someone who's supposed to be me, living this nightmare. But feeling like I know it's not really me, because nothing like this is supposed to, or is even capable, of happening. Does that make sense? Like being in a dream but somehow recognizing you're in one. It makes me angry this isn't just a nightmare for you to wake up from and be done with.

Anger: At some point anger settles in and you may not even realize it. You may be angry at your loved one, friends, family, God, people that you did not hear from or who disappointed you when your loved one died. You may find yourself responding angrily to someone you love that is helping you. Your anger is not always rational but underneath that anger is your pain. You feel lost, abandoned, and not so sure what to do with all that pain. I remember sitting with my grief counselor one day and saying to her "Oh my God, I think I am officially in the angry stage." I knew I needed to apologize to my family and friends that I may have directed my anger towards.

From my journal:

I think I am officially in the angry phase.....I came to that realization while I was with my counselor the other night and it is not a fun place to be. I feel sorry for everyone around me so I apologize in advance. Once again everyone, thank you for standing by me through this journey; you all mean the world to me.

Bargaining: This is when we may bargain with God that if only we can have our loved one back, we will never be angry with them again or we will only do great things with the rest of our lives if only we can have them back. This is a stage I do not recall going through and if I did, I did not recognize it. According to Ross and Kessler in, *On Grief and Grieving*, "the stages are responses to feelings that can last for minutes or hours as we flip in and out of one and then another." "We do not enter and leave each individual stage in a linear fashion. We may feel one, then another and back to the first one."

Depression: We are feeling empty and the pain is getting deeper. We think this will last forever. We may think there is no point in going on. We may not think we have the strength to go on. We ask our loved one for guidance. We may think it would be better if we joined them. This stage is difficult and checking in with your physician is important especially during this stage. Medication may be appropriate for some people. Grief counseling is very helpful in this stage. It is important to do whatever we need to do to get through this stage and it will be different for each of us.

Acceptance: In this stage we are coming to the understanding that our loved one is really physically gone and now we need to figure out a way to be a part of this world without them. We are still not alright that this happened and we will never like it but have reluctantly come to the conclusion that it is our new reality. This process can take a very long time. For me, it came only after navigating through the second anniversary of my husband's death.

Author David Kessler writes, "In our work, *On Grief and Grieving,* Elisabeth Kubler-Ross and I wanted to revisit the stages for clarification in grief and loss. The stages have evolved since their introduction and they have been very misunderstood over the past three decades. They were never meant to help tuck messy emotions into neat packages. They are responses to loss that many people have, but there is not a typical response to loss as there is no typical loss. Our grief is as individual as our lives."

As much as I resisted that these stages might apply to me, I did come to realize that what I was feeling and thinking was actually   appropriately described in the stages of grief and giving them a name was helpful to me.

The Deep Dark Hole

It was a Friday eight weeks after my husband's death. He died on a Friday.

I was working in my local office that day. That is where I was when I got "the call."

I was driving his truck for the first time. He died in his truck.

It was the perfect storm.

I should have stayed home that day. I was so sad and exhausted and things were not going well at work. Perhaps I had returned to work too early; perhaps I was not ready to be working full time.

Who was I to be making these decisions anyway? I had no experience with profound loss. I could not think straight let alone make decisions like how long I should stay out of work and how many hours I should work. I wanted to do the right thing. I wanted to be responsible, I wanted to keep busy and not be so sad all the time.

The problem was that the grief was still so fresh. At some point that morning, it all caught up with me, the sadness, the loneliness, the confusion about what I should do. I still had a very hard time focusing on work. I spoke to my supervisor and we agreed I should go home and that moving forward, I would work fewer hours.

Of course I had to drive the truck home. By the time I reached my house I was overwhelmed with sadness. I had pain in the very depth of my soul and I could not manage my grief. I felt like I was spinning out of control. I thought I could not go on any longer, that living without my husband was not going to work for me. If only someone could just give me a shot and knock me out so I did not have to feel this way, I would welcome that. I would welcome being in a coma until the pain was gone.

I felt like I was in a deep dark hole, a deep pit like the one in the movie *The Silence of the Lambs*. No one could help me, no one could see me, no one could possibly understand. What was the point? I could not go on. I could not manage this grief anymore. It was just too hard.

What should I do? I had no answers. At some point I managed to call my sister and ask her to please come and be with me. She of course came right away. She had never seen anyone like this before. She had never seen me like this. She was not sure how to help. Think of happy things she said; think of your family, your grandchildren. I said this is so much bigger than that. I cannot see my way out of this. I am not looking at my world the way you and everyone else is. I see nothing but darkness.

For the first time in my life, I had just a glimpse of what depression must feel like. It was scary. Everything was dark. I could see no way out of the pit, the "Deep Dark Hole." I could not see anything but pain, sadness, and despair.

For hours my sister sat with me while I cried. Why was this happening? Why was I suffering so much? How would I go on? Should I go on?

None of the things that usually helped me manage my grief were working today. This was so big. I began to think I would feel like this forever and that scared me.

After about seven hours, I was exhausted to the point where I could not fight my way out of the pit any longer. I would collapse there until I found the strength to climb my way out. At some point due to pure physical and emotional exhaustion, I fell asleep.

Eventually I reached a turning point. I managed to climb out of the deep dark hole. I will never know exactly how that happened, and I pray that I never enter that place again!

I would continue the fight. I would work harder. I would find the strength. I would go on.

Dreams

When I lost my husband, I stopped having dreams. It was largely due to the fact that I did not sleep much at all for the first year. I did not want to dream about my husband. I was not ready to dream about him. For me that meant he was in the past and he would never be back. The thought of accepting that scared me.

My first dream came fourteen months after I lost my husband. All the people and things he loved were incorporated into the dream. It was like he had just been away on a trip. It was never clear in my dream where he had been but I was so happy he was back, that it did not matter! Then I awoke and had to face my new reality! Today would be a really bad day.

Facing Your Fears

When I lost my husband, my self-confidence and sense of security were shaken. I no longer had that one person who would always be in my corner, someone I could share my innermost thoughts with, someone who would always have my back. Despite the help and support of family and friends, at the end of the day, I was always alone.

From Marian:

All the loving people you have in your life give you a safe container for all your feelings, but cannot absorb them or take them away.

Fighting grief can be a daunting task. You feel like a warrior heading to battle. You have to wear your armor all the time because you never know when there will be a sneak attack. It takes you by surprise and you never feel ready for battle.

Going places for the first time, seeing people for the first time, doing things alone for the first time all represented fear to me.

The fear of seeing people he knew, people I know, people we both knew was overwhelming and anxiety provoking. What would I say, what would they say? Would they say anything? Or would they avoid me? Would they pity me?

For me, it was just easier not to face these fears. I called upon family and friends to do some of these things for me. I went to new grocery stores, new gas stations, and new shops. I found different ways to get things done.

This system worked for me for a long time but I knew at some point, I needed to face my fears.

Gradually I started facing one fear at a time. Each time I faced a fear and survived it, it gave me the strength and courage to continue.

The Trip

As I started gaining strength and courage in facing my fears, I was invited to a wedding. My cousin's daughter was getting married. Not such a big deal you may be thinking, but this wedding was taking place in London, England and I live in Maine.

My cousin Andrew and his wife, Maria travelled from England to Maine to attend my son's wedding, and I thought how nice it would be if I could return the gesture.

My Dad was from England so I have been there a few times and I am very close to my English family. I discussed it with my sons and they agreed that while it would be a huge fear to face, in the end it would be good for me. I promised my dad before he died that I would always stay connected to our family in England and I decided this would be a great way not only to overcome a fear, but also to honor my Dad.

I worked through my fear and anxiety and made the decision to go on the trip. I contacted my travel agent to make the arrangements. I reached out to my cousin and he was excited that I would be attending the wedding. We stayed in touch during the planning stage and that was reassuring to me. After some trepidation during the planning, the pieces started coming together and I found myself looking forward to the trip.

I arrived in London on schedule with my family there to greet me. My husband would be happy and proud to know that I was facing my fears. The wedding took place on my birthday. One of the readings at the ceremony was a poem that was very important to me. I knew in my heart that this trip was meant to be. I was glad that I had overcome my fear and decided to go. I was proud to honor my Dad and represent our family at the wedding.

Poem by E.E. Cummings

i carry your heart with me
i carry your heart with me (i carry it in
my heart) i am never without it (anywhere
i go you go, my dear; and whatever is done
by only me is your doing, my darling)
                              i fear
no fate (for you are my fate, my sweet) i want
no world (for beautiful you are my world, my true)
and it's you are whatever a moon has always meant
and whatever a sun will always sing is you

here is the deepest secret nobody knows
(here is the root of the root and the bud of the bud
and the sky of the sky of a tree called life; which grows
higher than the soul can hope or mind can hide)
and this is the wonder that's keeping the stars apart

i carry your heart (i carry it in my heart)

This poem has a special meaning for me. On my husband's birthday that year, I bought a necklace that had a small heart inside a larger heart and for me that signifies that even though he is no longer physically with me, I will always carry his heart in my heart. He is always with me. Just that morning, I told my cousin Marion about the necklace and the poem. When we heard the poem read at the wedding ceremony, we looked at each other and realized it was a very special moment.

The Empty Chair

In January, four months after my husband died, it was time to celebrate my twin sons' thirtieth birthday. Birthdays are a time to reflect the years of joy your children have given you and to admire the fine young men they have become. For parents it is a time to be proud and to realize the benefits of the hard work that goes into raising children.

We decided to go out to dinner as a family to celebrate the event. For me and my sons it was met with mixed emotion. We were all excited they were turning 30 and celebrating their accomplishments in life, yet it was the first birthday celebration that would take place without their Dad.

I had to be strong and face my fear of being out in public. I would do this for my sons. It was their day and fortunately they were able to be caught up in the moment.

When we arrived at the restaurant and were seated, I realized there was an empty chair next to me. The sight of this empty chair was a sad reminder that someone important was missing from this celebration. This would be the beginning of celebrating many events with an empty chair.

From the book "Daily Inspiration"

But maybe the loved one's presence is here, too in the care we take of each other, in the tenderness with which we try to fill the unfillable shoes.

From my son Brian:

I do think about this being the first year without Dad; the first birthday for us, for him, for you. There are other firsts we will encounter throughout the year. We will get through them together, we will support each other when we need it, and we will end up okay. I love you Mom, thank you so much for being the best mom I could ask for. You and Dad did a great job, and I hope you know that we're as proud that you two are our parents as you are of us to be your sons.

Holidays

Holidays are about families and friends sharing love, laughter, togetherness, and good food. I was blessed to have all of these things for so many years thus taking for granted that I would always have that.

Grief and loss have changed that. My husband and I loved hosting Thanksgiving. We each had our duties and pulled everything together. We looked forward to having our families join us.

Some years when everyone was full and sleepy, we played board games. We talked and told stories and shared memories of past holidays. After everyone left, my husband and I always sat and talked about how nice it was to have everyone together in our home. We knew we had a lot to be thankful for.

Now that I am alone I have a different perspective on holidays. It seems they are designed for people who fit into a particular design.

When you deviate from that design whether it is divorce, estrangement, conflict, or loss, the holidays are different. They serve as a reminder that things in your life are different than the story book version. Someone very important is missing from the celebration.

It takes more and more work to achieve any sense of happiness during the holidays. The hype surrounding them signifies an expectation that is difficult to achieve if you do not fit into a certain mold.

I am blessed and thankful to have a wonderful family and many friends that surround me during the holidays, but my view has forever changed.

From my brother Richard:

The cups for me symbolize the times we have spent over coffee, talking about the grieving process. I am not sure you fully realize how much these discussions have meant to me and my own grieving. The Holidays will be tough for you and I am struggling to know what to do or say. You have been an immense help guiding me through this process. So I may be looking to you for guidance.

For me, the loss is hovering over me before, during, and after the holiday. I am constantly reminded of what I lost. I try so hard to be "normal" for my family but that takes an exorbitant amount of energy and exhausts me both emotionally and physically.

From my journal after my first Christmas:

I felt like I was not supposed to engage in Christmas because it would be a betrayal to my husband. Next Christmas, I may just run away.

Friends

I am fortunate to have many friends that help me navigate through my grief. They have been there for me each step of the way.

Even after a year went by and I faced my second go around with the holiday season, my friends were there. They called, sent cards, e-mailed, texted, and let me know they were thinking of me as I approached another holiday season without my husband.

When my husband died (it is still hard to write that word) four of my friends travelled from Florida to Maine to be with me at different times. That was an incredible gift of friendship!

My co-workers were there to console me when I returned to work, to take me to lunch, to listen, to cry with me, to bring me flowers, plants, candles, and soup.

I sometimes wonder how it must be for people who do not have friends and family to help them through their journey. When people I know lose a loved one, I make it a point to reach out and pay forward all the love and support I received. It is the least I can do.

Some Friendships Change

Not everyone will be able to give you what you need in your time of grief. People do things for their own reasons. I learned in my grief work that if your friends cannot give you what you need, you can distance yourself from them until you feel better.

A very wise friend of mine told me: "Some of your friendships will change, some will become stronger, and some will just be different." Those words resonated with me. Some indeed have become stronger and some are indeed just different. That is all right. It is how it has to be. I cherish the ones that have grown stronger and I honor the ones that have just changed.

From Toni:

The grief of suddenly losing your spouse is a wound that heals at its own speed. Linda is fortunate to have an awesome team and we are all aware that it is a long journey, and all we can do is be present, not forget her, recognize the small baby steps, and offer an ear to listen. She would do the same for us.

My Photo of the Day Gift

From Toni:

I usually go to Maine to relax and immerse myself in the beautiful scenery, it is their nature therapy. This year our trip was suddenly changed by the death of my dear friend's husband. Getting to Maine now was now about helping to console; being there to help in any way I could. All the compassionate care that I learned as an oncology massage therapist was now being put to the test on a much more personal level. All I wanted to do was help in any way I could and say the right thing at the right moment. All I felt that I could do was to listen: no way that I could relate.

During the time I spent with her I pulled out all the tools in my toolbox for compassionate care: hugs, sitting quietly, working very hard at not saying something insensitive.

What a job Toni had just being in the house with me during this time of intense sadness and pain. There are no directions for helping someone through grief. It is very much trial and error.

One day Toni announced that she would commit to sending me a photo every day for one whole year. At the time, I was in such a difficult place, I did not think too much of it. She always took great photos and frequently shared them with me. I always enjoyed her photos but now I was not sure if I could enjoy anything.

From Toni:

Leaving was very difficult, I knew I needed to do something to keep her "in my mind" and let us stay connected long distance. I made a commitment for one year to stay in touch with nature photography that I had taken over the years. Nature therapy with compassion, it was the least that I could do.

Little did I know then just how poignant this act of friendship would be! I looked forward to the photos each day. Toni worked hard to make the photos pertinent— to connect them to what I was feeling or going through at the time. I was not sleeping much and was up very early. Fortunately, Toni gets up early too so the photos arrived early and as much as I liked the photos, I also loved corresponding with her.

We would write back and forth and we decided that even though we lived far apart (she in Florida), we were having our morning coffee together. It became my form of journaling and my way to start my day with a friend.

I missed having my husband to talk to in the morning. I spilled my guts to her every single day. It was therapeutic for me. I was sometimes sad, sometimes cranky, utterly exhausted, frustrated, angry, and every other emotion you can imagine. I went through them all. She never gave up on me. She never took my crankiness personally. She was receptive to learning how to help me, what worked, what did not.

We even had a photo I could use when I just could not talk or even answer e-mails. I could send out the warning flag and Toni would know what that meant and that would ease her mind because when she did not hear from me, she worried.

When we talked, in addition to how I was progressing, we also discussed what was going on with her and that was a good distraction for me. Focusing on someone else was therapeutic. I hoped that at times, I was helping her just a little.

How do you possibly thank someone for such a gift? She kept her promise and sent a photo each and every day for an entire year. It was one of the kindest, most compassionate gifts of friendship I could ever receive. It may not have seemed like a big deal to her, but it meant the world to me.

How Do You Get to Heaven?

I am blessed to have three granddaughters that bring so much love and joy to my heart. They have been good medicine for me since I lost my husband or "Beepa" as he was known to them. They speak of him often and my son and daughter-in-law do their best to keep him in their hearts.

At the cemetery, the oldest, Emily who was four at the time would not leave my side. She has always been able to connect to my feelings and she knew this was a sad day.

A week or so later when I visited their house, Emily approached me. It was clear that she had been thinking about what she was going to say which is amazing for a four year old. She put her arms around me and said, "Nan, I miss Beepa a lot!" It was a special moment between us—happy and sad all at the same time.

One day when my son, the three girls and I went to the

playground, the three year old, Madeline started walking away. When my son asked her where she was going, she said, "I am going to heaven to see Beepa." In the mind of a three year old, heaven is a place you can go to and visit people.

Shortly after the two year anniversary, Emily randomly decided to write a message on a balloon and send it to heaven. She wrote, "Deer Beepa, I love you, I miss you. When my son sent me that photo, I cried but in a good way. It warmed my heart.

My youngest granddaughter, Julia, was only one when my husband died. She never got a chance to get to know him. We have all made it a point to talk to her about him and when we do, she always says "I miss Beepa too."

Each September, on the anniversary of my husband's death, we make a trip to the cemetery. The girls decorate their own small pumpkin and place it by the stone. It is a very sweet thing to watch. My husband would love that so much. He adored those girls.

There Are Days

From my journal:

It is hard to believe that an entire year has passed since you were taken from me. There are days that I still cannot accept it emotionally. After all, it happened in the blink of an eye! There was no warning, no preparing, no time to say goodbye.

There are days that I come home and see your truck in the driveway and think, maybe it was all just a bad dream, and you are back. Then reality hits me.

There are days I cannot bear the pain and sadness and think, as wonderful as everyone has been to me they cannot possibly understand exactly how it feels and how at the end of every day, I am alone.

There are days I just do not want to do this anymore and think it is too hard and takes too much energy.

There are days I feel a spark of joy and think maybe I will feel "normal" again someday.

There are days I want to sell the house and move to another town and not have painful reminders.

There are days I want to stay in this house with its wonderful memories and reminders of you.

There are days I feel hopeless and then there are days I feel hope.

There are days…………..and I must face them one at a time

Coming Home

As difficult as it was going back to work, it sometimes served as a good distraction. After all, my husband was never at work with me. No one had their spouse at work so I was on even ground. Getting ready in the morning was what I had always done. It felt normal.

During my work day, I had to get things done. This meant thinking about the task at hand and trying to block out the sadness with distractions.

When it was time to go home is when things got tough. I would feel anxious knowing the reality I was going home to. Some days I would work late just to avoid going home or stop by a friend's house or go to the mall, anything to avoid going home to an empty house.

When I did arrive home, feelings of anxiety came over me. I had to put lights on right away and I needed noise. The empty house was too quiet so I put on the television just to have noise in the house.

Dinner time was always the hardest and I would calm down as it got closer to bedtime knowing that I made it through another day yet knowing it would start all over again tomorrow!

I Hate Roller Coasters

I feel like I was taken to an amusement park and put on a roller coaster and no one will let me off. I do not even like roller coasters. As a matter of fact, I hate roller coasters.

I scream please, please let me off, I am scared, I am nervous; I do not want to be on this ride. No one asked me if I wanted to do this, no one is listening to my screams, my cries, my panic, and my pleas.

I didn't plan to be by myself at this point in my life. After 31 years of marriage, it did not occur to me that I would be alone.

But then that sounds so crazy doesn't it? Life is short and life is not always fair, so why did I think that my life would be different?

What about our sons? Their dad was their go-to person. He knew so much about so many things. Who will they talk to about politics? Who will they talk to about sports, old cars, music, genealogy, history?

What about the rest of my life? What do I do now? What plans do I make? Where do I go?

So many decisions to make! How can I make them? I am not equipped to make all these decisions.

Please send me back to level ground, where my feet are planted, where I feel safe, where my husband is.

Finally after a very long time they let me off the ride. I feel lost, where am I? Where have I been? Where is my husband? He will know what to do.

But the truth is my husband is no longer here. I am now alone on this roller coaster of life.

Grief Toolkit

In the early stages you are so raw you just are not sure what to do. Friends and family make suggestions and you think; I cannot process what you are saying. It is all I can do to get up and get dressed each day.

I found that if I put everything in my toolbox, perhaps when I was alone and feeling sad, I would pull something out of the box and give it a try.

The things that help you get through may be different than the things that helped me however I am sharing them with the hope that just one of them may help you feel better if only just for one moment. If that is the case, I know you will cherish that peaceful moment.

One day when I was feeling particularly sad, I received a book in the mail. It was from Robin, a co-worker. It was a book called *Tear Soup* by Pat Schwiebert and Chuck DeKlyen. I read the book and found that it made me feel better for a little while. This book would become an important part of my grief work.

Robin may never realize the significance of that gift. It said all the things I was thinking in a simple but elegant manner. I began reading this book several times a day during those times when I felt panicky and the pain was deep in my soul. It became one of my go-to tools.

At one point, I reached out to the author to let her know how much *Tear Soup* helped me and that I too was writing a book about grief. She responded and thanked me for my kind words and said, "You will be surprised by how many people your book will help."

For Your Toolkit

If you are grieving:

Grief Counselor: Find the right one for you.

Compassion hotline: Available 24 hours a day.

Support Group: Specific to your loss

Grief CD's: To calm the anxiety inside you.

Journaling: Put your feelings into words.

Books on Grief: Find the ones that resonate.

Internet resources: Choose the ones that speak to you.

Family and friends: Have a call list available.

Songs: My favorite is, "Keep me in your heart" by Warren Zevon

If you are helping someone through grief:

Books: Choose the ones that connect to their grief.

<u>Books that helped me include</u>:

On Grief and Grieving: Finding the Meaning of Grief through the Five Stages of Loss by Kübler-Ross, Elisabeth, and David Kessler.

Tear Soup: A Recipe for Healing after Loss by Pat Schwiebert and Chuck De Klyen

Writing to Heal the Soul by Susan Zimmerman

When Prayers Aren't Answered by John E. Welshons

Healing After Loss Daily Medications for Working Through Grief by Martha Whitmore Hickman

Here If You Need Me by Kate Braestrup

Grief Therapy by Karen Katafiasz

Stay in touch: Keep the cards, calls, texts, and e-mails coming. If they cannot take your call, they will not. They will be comforted just to know you are thinking of them.

Ocean walks: A walk on the ocean with a friend can be therapeutic.

Spa certificates: A professional massage can calm aching muscles associated with grief fatigue and calm the sad thoughts.

Errands: Offer to do them or accompany them on errands. There is no energy to do these tasks.

Gifts of food: There were days I would not have eaten if not for the delivery of nutritious frozen meals I received.

And most importantly:

"Please bring soup."

Some foods provide solace as much as they do nourishment. Soup is one of those foods for me. It evokes a feeling of comfort inside me.

From Toni:

"Well, I believe your book needs a chicken soup recipe to signify the importance of doing something for someone when you are not sure what to do. The time spent in the kitchen quietly cutting and chopping and being in a space that is sacred. The kitchen was the safe place for me to be; I knew that from the start and you made me feel comfortable when you voiced it."

"I am someone who needs a task, and cooking made it possible to help. So much energy draining out; food is a way I thought I could help."

The soup should be nutritious, filled with vegetables that have a variety of medicinal and nutritional effects:

Onions: known to have antiviral properties.

Celery: a good source of vitamin C, which helps to support the immune system and reduce cold symptoms.

Carrots: loaded with beta-carotene; pro vitamin A.

Oregano: season with oregano; it is loaded with antioxidants.

Chicken: let's not forget the chicken-a good source of protein.

When all these ingredients are chopped, deboned, and simmered together, the smell stimulates your limbic system, which is your emotional brain. You remember the times a bowl of chicken soup was lovingly made to make you feel better.

As the months went on, more people made chicken soup for me and one friend makes it for me on each anniversary. I do not think anyone realizes how meaningful the gift of **"chicken soup" is for me, so comforting and so compassionate.**

The Details of Death

When someone dies, there is so much paperwork. There are phone calls to make, death certificates to send out. Carrying around a piece of paper that officially says your loved one is dead can be devastating, yet so many places require this "proof of death."

One of the things that distressed me was going online and removing my husband's name from our accounts. It was especially difficult to remove him as my emergency contact person and beneficiary.

When doing this online, I literally had to hit the "delete button" It felt so wrong and disrespectful. How could he be removed that easily? He was too important in so many lives to be deleted.

Organ Donation

When we got back home on that fateful day, I received a call about organ donation. My husband was on the donor list yet I was not ready to talk about it on that day. I knew that organ donation is something that has to happen quickly. Thankfully, my son was there to help me with this difficult call.

It was all very overwhelming. I got a sense of what that is like for other families. On the worst day of their life when they are immersed in the horror of the death of a loved one, they are asked about donating a part of that loved one. It all seems surreal.

No one feels prepared to make such a decision and now I can understand why it is so important to have that discussion when we are alive and to sign a donor card. I am not sure I would have been able to go to that place given the circumstances of my husband's death. I am grateful that he made his own decision and as a family, we wanted to honor that.

As a nurse who works with people that have kidney failure and are awaiting kidney transplants, I am aware of the significance of organ donation.

When I started receiving correspondence from the organ bank, it was met with conflicting feelings. Part of me was still reeling from the loss and I could not fully process this gift he made or what it meant. At the time, I could not appreciate what the organ bank was sending me.

But when I received a letter from a recipient that the organ bank forwarded to me, it all became clear. Jim's gift, our gift was now helping someone. I was hearing first-hand what that meant and how appreciated it was by the recipient and his family.

Organ donation is a very powerful experience for both the donor family and the recipient family. The organ bank never forgets that. They follow up with cards, books, and letters. They make sure you know how much your gift meant to someone and how much it is appreciated.

So your worst moment can become someone else's best moment and there goes the cycle of life.

From the Recipient

Dear Donor Family,

"It has been one month since I had surgery in which the tissue your loved one so generously donated was used. I want to express my sincere thanks and gratitude for this kind gift. I am very sorry for your loss and I know it must be very hard to live without them. I hope you can find some comfort in knowing my life has changed because of their generosity and compassion. As a result of experiencing this act of kindness, I too have elected to become an organ donor so that I may also help someone in need"

Thank God We Did That

When you lose someone you love suddenly and unexpectedly, you immediately think about the things you have done, should have done, have said, or should have said. With sudden death, you do not get any more chances to say "I love you" or tell your loved one what they meant to you. The end is written and now that is your story.

Fortunately for me and my family, we had a lot of "Thank God we did that" memories. The Sunday before my husband died, we took our son, daughter-in-law, and their three girls to Storyland. It was a great family day for all of us and watching the girls have so much fun brought joy to my husband and me.

The evening before my husband died, my son e-mailed the photos from Storyland. I remember my husband telling me that he received the e-mail with the photos. He was thrilled to look at them.

The Saturday before he died, his sister and her husband spent the day with us at our cabin on the lake. We had lots of laughs and to this day, the three of us talk about how glad we are to have that memory.

The month before he died, we spent time with good friends in Rhode Island. We caught up with what was happening in our lives; with our children and enjoyed a picnic at the ocean.

The next day, we spent the day with our son and his new girlfriend in Boston. We enjoyed getting to know her and took a trip on a duck boat.

A few weeks before he died, my husband went to a Boston Red Sox game with our son. It was a game that had been rained out in the spring and rescheduled. They had green monster tickets which is a big deal at Fenway Park. It was a thrill for both of them! I remember that my son sent photos on that special day he spent with his Dad.

The Tuesday before he died, he and I spent the evening at our cabin on the lake getting it ready for our son and his girlfriend who were planning to spend a relaxing weekend at the cabin. Spending time there was such a joy for both of us. We enjoyed the peace and quiet of the lake. Little did I know it would be the very last time we would spend time there together. Thank God we did that!

From my journal:

Jim, thank God we took that trip to the Bahamas eight months before you died. It was just the two of us and it was the most relaxing, enjoyable vacation we ever had. I am so glad I have that memory to hold onto.

Decisions

In the early days of grief, you do not feel confident to make decisions. Grief literature actually suggests that you should not make any major decisions for two years.

For me, it was not difficult to comply with this recommendation. I did not feel capable or competent to make decisions like selling property or moving. I was now also the "man of the house" making all the decisions and it was all I could do to keep up with what I had to do on a day to day basis.

When I reached the two year mark, I started feeling more capable to make decisions. One important aspect to consider when making important life decisions is thinking about how you will feel afterward.

Historically, I put a lot of thought into my decisions so that when I make them, I will not have regrets. This was now even more important! When your lose your life-partner and have to make all the important decisions on your own, you want to make sure you continue to honor that person, and feel safe and secure with the outcome of your decisions.

For me, when the time was right, the ideas would just come to me. I may have casually been thinking about doing some of these things but then like a ton of bricks, I would just feel something telling me it was time to do it.

I like to think my husband is helping me make these decisions in some way, shape, or form.

When the Time is Right

What do you do with your loved one's possessions? This is a very difficult decision for all of us who have suffered loss. Since my loss is that of a spouse, I am sharing how that worked and continues to work for me.

Having your spouse's belongings is a mixed blessing. While it stirs up painful memories and reminders that sting, it also allows you to feel close to that person whether it is a piece of clothing or one of their special possessions.

You will experience a variety of feelings. There is some guilt when you part with their possessions, there is sadness, and there is the feeling that you are putting them in the past. No one can fully understand what that is like until and unless they have experienced it.

Friends and family may have suggestions for you and may want some of those treasures. I found that if my sons wanted some of their dad's things, it touched my heart.

There were things that I needed out of my house immediately. Things that were so important to my husband like the antique truck he bought just two weeks prior to his death. He loved that truck and pulled it out of the garage at night just to admire it! We sold the truck right away because it was too painful to look at it every single day.

For everything else, I followed my heart and kept things until I felt capable of making a decision that I would not regret. I had to trust that I would know when the time was right and trust myself to make the right decision for me and my family.

From a friend:

When my ten year old nephew died, people told my sister she needed to get his things out of the house. This hurt her so much. How could they be so insensitive?

For Those Who Come After You

Not long after my husband died, I had an appointment with my primary care physician. I was still feeling so sad. I had no energy. I remember her telling me that one of the best ways to help myself feel better was to help someone else. I recall thinking, "What is wrong with her? Doesn't she realize how sad and distraught I am? I am a mess so how can I possibly help someone else?"

When you experience profound loss, you become an expert in grief by virtue of your own experience. It is hard to think of it that way, However you start to find that you can be a comfort to those who come after you. You can listen to them describe their pain and feel a connection because while their circumstance may be different, people who experience that type of loss understand that the pain reaches deep into the soul and is pretty much not imaginable unless you have experienced it.

I found myself reaching out to those who came after me and feeling comfortable listening to their stories and feeling that I was providing them some small comfort which I knew was a gift. I was fortunate enough to have received that gift and now it was my turn to give it to someone else.

One day when I was feeling particularly lonely and sorry for myself, the phone rang. It was an eighty-eight year old woman I know. She lives in a retirement center. She lost her husband many years ago. She still misses him and talks about him and feels that she can understand what I am going through. I believe she can.

She does not live close to her children and I know that is difficult for her. I cannot imagine what that is like especially at her age.

During our conversation, I could tell she was feeling lonely and sad. As she aged, her health was deteriorating and she was not able to get out and do things.

I shifted from feeling sorry for myself to trying to help her feel better. I knew she was calling me because she needed someone to talk to today. She was always good about checking in on me after my husband died. Today, I knew I could help her. I feel that our chat lifted her spirits on this particular day.

When I got off the phone, I knew I had helped to make someone's day better and at the same time shift the focus off myself. She does not know it, but her call came at just the right time. It was what we both needed that day.

When you start to feel lonely and sad, pick up the phone or visit someone that you know is struggling with a difficult life circumstance and you will realize that is the best medicine for your grieving soul. I decided that my physician gave me very good advice in those early days of grief.

It Takes a Team

Without the love and support of my family and friends I may not have been able to get to the other side of grief. The role they played and continue to play is difficult to explain. How do you find the words to let people know that their actions, love and kindness got you through the worst time of your life?

I did not have to look very far to find family, friends, and co-workers to help me. Day or night they were there to hold my hand, wipe my tears, give me a hug, sit with me, cook for me, take me to the ocean, take me to do my errands , take me to lunch or invite me for a meal. They called, they visited, they e-mailed and texted, sent cards, sent books, sent flowers, sent gifts.

When I could not stand to be alone, they were there. When I needed to talk, they were there. When I needed a hug, they were there. They came from near and far.

I knew I was fortunate to have this team of people ready and willing to help me through the pain. I was so vulnerable and I just could not bear to be alone.

At some point, I worried that my friends and family would tire of me and become inpatient but of course that did not happen.

Many people on my team have told me that they got as much from me as I got from them and that touched my heart. We talked about more than grief and on those occasions, I was able to take a break from my sadness. Knowing that this was not just a one-way street; that we were in it together; and that everyone was learning many lessons about life and grief was comforting to me.

From my journal:

I have never in my life felt so vulnerable. It is a very uncomfortable feeling. I believe you all know me as a strong independent person but at this time, I do not feel very strong. As we navigate through our grief together we will all inevitably take many poignant life lessons with us.

The People Mover

I feel like I was placed on a people mover, strapped in and forced to pass through holidays, birthdays, and special events that we celebrated together and I was not allowed to jump off.

I plead to be let off because I cannot take the pain and sadness that accompany the special events. But the people mover keeps on going all the way through year one. I feel grateful that I made it through year one and yell "please let me off now, this is enough" then a little voice says "year two is not so easy either" and here I go again. I fasten my seat belt and somehow get to the second anniversary. Thank goodness, the people mover finally slows down and comes to a stop. I look back and think of all the special days I made it through and realize that maybe I am as strong as my friends and family say I am.

From the book Grief Therapy:

Undertake new activities and create new rituals out of the past. Through them you can maintain the memory of your loved one, even as you embark on a different chapter in your life.

Creating a New Life

From Marian, my hospice chaplain and volunteer:

"Each of us is here, at this very moment—our hearts beating, our breath flowing—because we have been granted the gift of human life. There's no accounting for it, really, but this gift of life is ours, yours and mine. And with life comes the blessed capacity to love another, and to be loved, shaping each other's lives in myriad and mysterious ways. In turn, with love inevitably comes loss and grief…what has been called the painful price we pay for loving. Two sides of one very precious coin. We may understand that death is part of the natural order of things, and yet when someone we love dies it feels deeply unnatural, thrusting us into a new and foreign land where everything is altered."

So it is inevitable that we respond with resistance. "No, no," we cry, "this can't be." We hold on tight, wanting nothing more than for this connection to remain permanent and intact. We may feel like we have lost an essential piece of ourselves, for none of us lives life in isolation, but as part of an interconnected web: pull one strand and our small corner of the web is torn.

To love deeply and ultimately to let go is life's most difficult, awesome, and inspiring challenge, I believe. In the words of poet Mary Oliver: "To live in this world, you must be able to do three things: to love what is mortal, to hold it against your bones knowing your own life depends on it, and when the time comes to let it go, to let it go." On the face of it, that seems impossible.

But that's when the amazing capacities of our human spirits rise, like the wild geese into flight. And grace happens. Blessedly over time, the landscape of grief grows more familiar, more hospitable. We learn to read the map of this new country, learn its language; encounter people who help us find our way. We discover that while the person we loved is now physically separated from us in death, our connection to them, the threads that binds us to them, remain alive through the power of memory and love. The essence of this person--what made them unique and precious to us may even become clearer and stronger over time, sustaining us in ways that we might never have imagined. Others reach out with kindness and compassion; we may discover a deepening of our faith in a flow and source of life that is greater than our own, however we come to know and name it.

In her book entitled *Safe Passage*, Molly Fumia writes: "The season of our grief is a [drawing in] time. We secure our windows to the world and stock our cupboards with what we need to sustain us. Carefully we rebuild our inner fire, and nestle in its warmth while the storm gradually passes awaiting the spring that will come as surely as the steady passage of the days."

This description of the grieving process very much aligns with my personal journey. Year one was hell, year two was not so great either.

I feel like I was put in a medically induced coma for two years and was taken out of it long enough to go to work and participate in a few activities and then back in I went. I was exhausted beyond imagination.

As I enter year three, the cloud of sadness is starting to lift. I am out of my coma. Sleep is coming a bit more regularly and I am starting to regain some of the energy I lost. I am getting back some of my confidence, trusting myself to make decisions, and feeling that I will make it after all.

From the book "Grief Therapy"

It may seem as if you'll never feel truly happy again. But be assured that you will and your joy will have richness and a depth that come from your having known profound pain and profound healing.

Year three will be a rebuilding year. I have to create a life without my husband. I am still trying to figure out exactly what that will look like however I remain hopeful and open to the possibilities.

I have reason to believe that someday I will be at peace, that I will be able to laugh and smile and be happy again. I will think of my husband and remember the life we had, the blessings we were given, and have peace in my heart rather than pain.

Acknowledgements

I personally wish to thank the following people without whom I may not have made it to the other side of grief. It is with your love and support that I was able to see the light at the end of the tunnel and complete this project.

To: my loving sons, Sean and Brian, for being there for me when they were also grieving and for reminding me that their Dad lives on in them.

To: my daughter-in-law Michelle for holding me together at the hospital that fateful day and helping the children remember "Beepa."

To: Lauren for embracing our family and connecting so lovingly to my pain and suffering.

To: my brother Richard and my sister Patricia for being there for me morning, noon, and night to do whatever I needed.

To: Jim's sister Jane and her husband Walter for staying with me when I needed people, and for feeding me when I may not have eaten.

To: my niece Jill for her love and support, for spending time with me, and for moving back to Maine at just the right time.

To: my extended family for reaching out to me with food, calls, e-mails, cards, and gifts.

To: my amazing group of friends, Toni, Barbara, Debi, Peggy, Pam, Deb, for going above and beyond and demonstrating that long term friendships are a gift to be treasured.

To: my co-workers for their generosity of time, lunches, books, cards, visits, and soup.

To: my cousin Sandy for knowing just what to say and do and being available when I needed her most.

To: my Hospice volunteer Marian, for her visits, compassion, and contribution to my book.

To: Jim, my writing coach for his support and encouragement in bringing this project to completion.

To: my fellow grievers for understanding and taking time from your grief to comfort me and share your stories.

Linda Andrews is a Registered Nurse. Her experience includes intensive care, pediatrics, and nephrology. She has shared end of life experiences with patients and their families. She has been

there to listen and to support people who are making decisions that will end their lives.

In September of 2011, Linda Andrews lost her father and just two weeks later, her husband. During this very difficult time, she came to the realization that many people in our society have difficulty responding to grief.

Please Bring Soup is Linda's first book. It's intended as a gift to others who have suffered loss. She offers suggestions that help both the grievers and those who are supporting them. Through her stories and journal entries, she describes the depth of pain that comes with profound loss, as well as sharing ideas about what helps and what does not.